Frida Kahlo Wakes Up to Find Diego Rivera in the Mood

poems by

Jessica Noyes McEntee

Finishing Line Press
Georgetown, Kentucky

Frida Kahlo Wakes Up to Find Diego Rivera in the Mood

ACKNOWLEDGMENTS

"Florida" was published in 2022 by *Streetlight Magazine*
"So I Gave It" was selected for an honorable mention in the 2019 3rd
Wednesday Poetry Contest

Publisher: Leah Huete de Maines

Editor: Christen Kincaid

Cover Art: Frissell, Toni, photographer. Frida Kahlo Senora Diego Rivera
standing next to an agave plant, during a photo shoot for Vogue magazine,
"Senoras of Mexico". Photograph. Retrieved from the Library of Congress,
<www.loc.gov/item/2013651904/>.

Author Photo: Jesse Gwilliam / Office of Communications Amherst College

Cover Design: Elizabeth Maines McCleavy

Order online: www.finishinglinepress.com
        also available on amazon.com

Author inquiries and mail orders:
Finishing Line Press
PO Box 1626
Georgetown, Kentucky 40324
USA

Contents

Frida Kahlo Wakes Up to Find Diego Rivera in the Mood

Spare me your six A.M. spin
about the magic of our corporeal beings,
how grated stars salt our saliva.
I know: your every excretion
spews a universe, the water strained
by my eyes once put the dew
on King Tut's tongue.

No. Give me a gray day so I can match it,
grieve the beggared body I must lug—
my spine an iron rose,
a brace made
for your guillotine.

Florida

This place emptied my father, sucking him through the tunnel of its straw. Four days into a farewell visit, and I've overdosed on sunlight, rousing the insomniac within. The grass is gravid with alligators; the air poses as sand; cars scaffold a melted wax of spent bugs. Everywhere, I see darkness edging, shadows twitching to keep pace—the gloom that magics the glass into mirror.

So I Gave It

Always, I'll recall
the night your question
shadowed me;
a rabble of cicadas beat
on inbuilt tambourines;
the air a four-cornered curtain—
smell of wet velvet, of wet dog, of glue;
the set of your face—
eyes open-caved,
your lips made of sunset—
awaiting an absolution
I alone
could give.

A Poet's Response to the Unbottled Genie

Allow me three eternal poems:
the first to scoop the dead
from buried kilns
where they slow-bake,
patching the gobs of their ash.
The next could blunt the thorns
laid near the bloom
of my daughter's night song.
The last shall hatch a heart,
shuddering the beats
of your name.

Insomnia

I.

Liminal, I'm a sheet
of bubbled glass—a sham
solid, too chaotic to seize
a solid's shape.
A silica housecat—at once asleep,
at once awake.

II.

From on high, I leer into the frigid fishbowl
of sleep. I watch
the twitching black—prey
for the correction. (Please!) Melt
my bones into a carbon
haze. Smelt my mind into a mesh
sleeve. Drip-filter dreams
from my daze.

III.

My body has become the lobster stalking
the octopus. I can sniff the pliant
flesh passing as sand.

IV.

Insomnia is the loneliness in a marriage
bed; the unconsummated affair. The impotent
lover on-the-sly. The ultimate ungettable lay.

For the Child Who Took My Father's Stead

I.   To the one with the scrape of sand in his hair, with ocean salting his eyes. Forged for compensation—the death dream, inverted. Born into blocked light.

II. Tin foil sculpture, we corroded you. Or maybe we pretold you; we wrung out all your stories. You were birthed beneath the boulder of our longing, your brow rounded by the saline drip. Lungs pancaked, all your pink was blued.

III. We serenade the hyacinth that crowns every spring, but who can say how it suffers the ascent. Who can say its purple hide is not a badge; its body not a bruise.

IV. Soil-footed, root-veined. Of course you dream of flight.

The Grand & Grim Continuum

One morning, I trod south
into a brookside glade
that spring had painted;
chlorophylled, caffeinated.

Gobsmacked, I traced
a serpentine path
of daffodils, crowns blunting
their bodies' verdigris blades.

I plodded in farther
and deeper, bobbing, my head
throbbing in the glinting rays,
and I fed the flowers
the bacon of my ankles.
Nature is hungry; no, voracious.
A gorgeous and seductive mouth.

Soon I sank-walked, staggering,
sowing a scarlet trail
of my seeds—
the grass, a sponge, yielded
and crunched, yielded and crunched;
the sound of life. A bottomless
web of bones buoyed
what scant remained of mine.

Forecasted

The day is a gossip—
rain palpitates
the clouds' heartbeats. The passing cars'
wipers thrum, a heaving
lungfish. A runner
passes, soaked
with sky, and I wonder about you.
Waiting, I lose my legs
inside a wool mouth; I long
to take a corkscrew to the ceiling—
to storm the bed.

Kourtney Kardashian Convenes a Gothic Rehearsal Dinner in Portofino

The bride-to-be dons a black minidress scarcely longer than a tunic, and she's festooned her bosom with an image of the virgin Mary, whose chin tucks low in modesty. She gives her husband-to-be an open-mouthed kiss as their children look on; statues. Kourtney's night-black veil is rimmed with indigo, a nod, doubtless, to the Renaissance artists who once sacrificed lapis lazuli in manufacturing blue paint, a shade they reserved—reverentially and exclusively—for the Holy Mother.

What I Picture When I See Pottery Barn Pilgrim Plates on a Clearance Rack

Famine flee-ers.
Salvation seekers stacked
inside a fetid hull; unmarried
bodies wedded. They pass
their days memorizing
the sea's bipolar ways. The stars
ebullate their path.

They ululate the first batch
of the luckless until grief guzzles
their tongues.
Soon, they admit: we who are quick
must dispose of the trash fast;
unblessed and unregretted.

Landing, they whiffle
on whittled legs. Penetrate
a thick-grown forest—
wherein they find a chorus
of more beastly dangers still.

The settlers wear
their wounds—maggot-bait; pitted
bodies their New World costumes.
The stars misspend
their shine.

Swimming Lesson

My body was taut—a violin's string—and I charged
into the Atlantic, breaking
through the wave-line, willfully
blind to the growing distance from the shore
where my mother sunned.
She despised the water. I dove in

between the pursed blue lips. My legs
landed on the sandy tongue,
and I vaulted myself up again, borrowing
its rhythm. The ocean swallowed
and regurgitated. The universe
was a language,
and I a native speaker.

A handful of strokes more,
and I saw only blue; I was far
from the shore and moving
farther—my toes no longer scratching

the below. The blue blackened, adopting
the shade of my mother's eyes.
I was of an age when I believed
she was omnipotent; she could mince
the puppet master's strings.
And, back then, I often told myself: whatever
the tide borrows, it polishes

and returns.
A fanciful sort, I had no basis
for these lies. My mother's sister had fallen
for the water's indigo lure, decades before.
I'd long known this without knowing it,
a splinter carted in the thick

of my heel. All around me became water. My heart
sloshed. I, too, was going to
vaporize; I was going to leave
my mother. I screwed my lids tight and beat
my legs. They evaporated
beneath me; sea foam.
Defeated, cold, I lay
prostrate and gave fate
its way. The sky above looked inert
and pale; a porcelain
sheet, reflecting.

First Trip Away from My Children

They stay with my mother three hundred and thirty-seven miles away. Distant enough to question them, I think while I doze against the rumbling breast of the passenger seat; to make them a mirage. Maybe I dreamed them. Maybe I drew them.

The light on Marco Island appears refined, as if shot through a prism, carving everything. Bathers toe their way into the surf; the turquoise quarters their bodies.

I order an absinthe.

Penelope: My Life in Three Stanzas

I. Borne by a wine-colored sea, I was riven against rocky shores.

II. I grew into a lush and filthy garden—ripened soil, airborne rot. Skin a twitching peat. My green veins retched into the inky, center-left void.

III. For ten years, I laid untouched, praying to the blade of time: come, prune me to the cane.

Basso Profundo

Mornings, my neighbors—the newlyweds—chaperone each other on the journey to their driveway. He dips her form into the well of his gaze, polishing her earlobes with words

of praise. We were that way, once: fluorescent, emulsified. You pirated me to treasure; eyes gone to eggs with desire. We were the basso profundo in the bullfrog's throat.

How I Came to Prefer the Penguins

Once I knew the polar bear who lived alone in Central Park Zoo. I thought of him as a colossus; then as Cyclops, trapped in an airier cave. No, a tottering belfry, I decided one Saturday at ten fourteen. I pictured an internal rope of gristle tethering the gudgeon pin of his skull to a bell hanging at his center point; it would clank back and forth, counterbalancing

his every step. He ignored me as I gaped in his direction. I'd often tilt my head down, listening for his music. Maybe it was too deep a pitch, for human ears—like earth music. I wondered

as I watched: What did *he* make of us? Did the aroma of our nape-sweat ever cause him to salivate? Could he sniff the snacks festering in our backpacks? Later, in bed at night, I sometimes thought: Did he ever laugh at our knock-knock jokes, or scoff at our commentaries? Did he root for the young, pimpled-necked teenager in heat, blinding his way through a first seduction? Did he mock the clamped-mouth, would-be fiancé: *Ya gonna say yes*

to a zoo proposal? What did he think of the toddler who stood on sentry, befouling his diaper—you could tell this from the cocked angle to his knees. Homo sapien in his natural habitat, a caption would read. He champed upon a hemorrhaging popsicle, which in turn dripped a second set of veins upon his forearms. It looked like someone had plucked out a portion of his nervous system with a darning needle, as if to say, *This is what I was telling you about.* In the background, oblivious to all of this—the bear glowered through inkwell eyes, stomping out the boundaries of his cathedral. Once, he'd had a partner who died, I overheard the zookeepers say, but he was all but guaranteed to maul any replacement bear they might gift him. He'd already forgotten how to pantomime the act of getting on, how to convince us he'd been redeemed or, at the very least, part-tamed. I couldn't help myself; I could see the scene as it would play out: the crowd congregating on the lower level before a twelve-foot-tall pane of glass that, on normal days, enabled us to surveil his swims. We'd grow louder, waiting for the introduction, the realest of all reality shows. The smaller, newer bear, would be slipped inside; instinctively, she'd shadow

a corner. He'd circle about her, feigning disinterest. Sensing no threat, he'd saunter, shaking the hairs on his arse; his basketball-sized paws would strike the simulated rock surface—so hard they'd produce sparks. He'd pivot. Descending, he'd gut her; it would take no more than a single swipe of his claws. He'd strip off the onion skin of her pelt, vivisecting her for us, the shrieking crowd. I watched

this in the theater of my mind, more than once, I admit. Until one day, a new tour guide narrated. "Gus loves nothing more than to eat a herring breakfast." The bear's name was Gus. Did *he* know that? I choked. "He's so cute," a child enthused, hurling an unspeakable insult. *What have you to say for yourself...*

Gus? I asked, aghast. Like an animal, he feigned ignorance.

Winter Song

Sing December's pale and lipless
sky. Sing a dram of swallowed sun
and an icicle's slow mizzle.
Sing oaks twittering
like just-plucked birds,
and the neighbor's pond scabbed
with blue. Sing black cataract nights, stretched,
and a glittered moonscape
of ice-cratered fields. Sing
chimneys respiring thistledown
tufts and sled hills carved
to veins. Sing
seeds quartering, deep
as secrets.

On Turning Forty-Four

Now I see how I should've donned
the ermine of my youth with more ease—
which is to say, I wish I'd winked back. Once
I thought a dazzling storm would drill
down on me. Because, why? I was flat, a dull
brown made for drinking. Now I see: I should've fermented
the stars; swelled myself on pilfered
booty; nursed my filmy roots. Redoubled,
I'd have grown thick-
stalked; bloomed resplendent.

The Taxidermist

My cat makes dolls of mice. I discover another one in my morning fog—I loom, blinking—and usher it into a dustpan. His obsidian eyes look watchful, and his tiny hands curl in a defense he can no longer give. He feels weightless, like he never existed.

I inter the mouse in an unweeded corner of the garden, where his predecessors serve as witness. Inside, the cat licks his sun-warmed paws and flexes spotless ivory scythes.

After Seeing a George de La Tour

The new neighbors
took possession
of the yellow Victorian
hedged in by dripping purple
water; wisteria. Inside,
I see their tattered cat
as he makes love to
a porcelain lamp,
the vased peonies.
The couple appears
neither friendly nor comely.
I spy the man
Dip his knees and scoop
up one end of the stroller, sparing
the wheels a puddle.
His body—a flame—glints
as it rises—and it lights
their babe, who shines
up, beatifying them.

Mid-Winter Thaw

A January wind flogged the splintering
front door. I found myself marooned
on a couch the shade of celadon, my outstretched
legs balancing the boomerang
of my little dog's chin,

which, in turn, vibrated and gyrated
while he slumbered—or, as the Brits say, kipped
or zizzed, both of which sounded—to my unrefined American
ear—dirty and hence

ever so alluring. He kipped me slowly
up against the crumbling castle wall
for thirty-seven whole minutes—we exhausted
a vat of clotted cream—one might enthuse.
Or: Babe, I want to zizz
your inner elbow over

and over again until it oozes.
It was mid-winter;
so, too, was I. Mid-life,
middle class; middling; however,
loved by my dog-
blanket; and, fitfully, by my slumbering
children, arranged overhead

in their beds like commas. A branch
beyond the window's eye
crackled. Snow licked
the ground. All too soon, it would sculpt
the land to marble, refining
a pitted and uneven yard.

Gods of the Upper Floors

Termites have dispatched
a wooden beam
that once bottomed
the front facade
of our two-hundred-year-old house,
advertising sunlight
to our basement squatters—
hermetic beings that worship us
when we blast into flip
the circuit breaker
or to clear the heater's lungs.
They feast upon the drifts our bodies
shed as snow;
they jitter as we fight
in rooms overhead.
Our thunder displants clouds
of dust from their sky.

A Deathbed Confession

There'd be no blue blazers, no chiffon scarves. No golf-talk, no kid-talk, nor crystal highballs gravitied down with bourbon, sinking us into my company-only couch. No—I couldn't abide to watch his penny loafers cross my threshold, to blind my way through the fog of his house-compliments; to listen to him, inventing small talk like a husband, polluting his breath with words, making himself common. No—I say, no—I wanted the untamed version of him, the lawless one, the pre-evolved. The flesh that rippled.

He scritch-scratched on my back door, on a moonless night; stars spotlighted the grain of his pelage. I dragged him down the seven stairs and into my garage, installing him atop the oil-shadow that slicked the left car bank. Pebbles of cat food crunched into his shoulder blades. A split-lipped baby pool proved a wretched gossip, twittering into corners grown dusky with cobwebs, and I scoured my windpipe with his name, his lovely name, carrying him around—afterwards, always—secreted, within.

Jessie Noyes McEntee hails from Philadelphia. She studied art history and English at Amherst College and cut her teeth professionally at John Wiley & Sons. She's provided editorial guidance and ghostwriting for clients in New York and Connecticut, and she teaches fiction writing at Westport Writers' Workshop in Westport, CT. She also works at Pequot Library in Southport, CT and served as Westport's second Poet Laureate. She lives with her husband and two teenagers. Her first chapbook, *Jackie O. Suffers Two Husbands and Other Poems*, was published by Finishing Line Press in 2019.